LOVED ONES WITH CHRONIC ILLNESS

Loved Ones With

Lacey Hilliard and
AnneMarie McClain

Published in the United States of America by Cherry Lake Publishing Group
Ann Arbor, Michigan
www.cherrylakepublishing.com

Reading Adviser: Beth Walker Gambro, MS, Ed., Reading Consultant, Yorkville, IL
Book Designer: Jen Wahi

Photo Credits: cover: © metamorworks/Shutterstock; page 5: © Chaay_Tee/Shutterstock; page 6–7: © Andrey_Popov/ Shutterstock ; page 8 (left): petite lili/Shutterstock; page 8 (right): VGstockstudio/Shutterstock; page 9: © JPC-PROD/ Shutterstock; page 10: © Monkey Business Images/Shutterstock; page 11 (top): © Art_Photo/Shutterstock; page 11 (bottom left): Tolikoff Photography/Shutterstock; page 11: (bottom right) © Andrey_Popov/Shutterstock; page 12: © Kleber Cordeiro/ Shutterstock; page 13: © MMD Creative/Shutterstock; page 14: © Photoroyalty/Shutterstock; page 16: © Tyler Olson/ Shutterstock; page 17: © PeopleImages.com – Yuri A/Shutterstock; page 18 (left): © bbernard/Shutterstock; page 18 (right): © Ground Picture/Shutterstock; page 19: © Paper Trident/Shutterstock; page 20–21: © Starocean/Shutterstock

CONTENTS

WHAT IS CHRONIC ILLNESS?

Chronic illness is a disease or medical condition. Many chronic illnesses last a year or longer. Grown-ups and kids may have chronic illnesses.

There are many chronic illnesses. Some are heart disease, cancer, asthma, diabetes, and kidney disease. Chronic fatigue syndrome, fibromyalgia, and Alzheimer's disease are others. Sometimes injury or stroke can lead to a chronic illness.

Vitiligo is another chronic illness someone could have. It is an autoimmune disorder that causes patches of skin to lose color.

5

WHAT PEOPLE WITH CHRONIC ILLNESS MIGHT EXPERIENCE

Having a chronic illness is different for each person. You often can't tell someone has one by looking at them.

It's important to know if someone has a chronic illness. Doctors can help. Sometimes it gets figured out fast. Sometimes people go to appointments and wait. Waiting can make people feel worried.

Make a Guess!

What kinds of questions are experts asking about chronic illnesses? What do you think their work looks like?

Some chronic illnesses may change the way a person lives. Some may not change much.

Diabetes is a chronic illness. Diabetes is when someone has too much sugar in their blood. **Insulin** is a **hormone** in your body. Insulin helps the body have the right amount of sugar. Diabetic people test their blood often. They check to see if they need more insulin. Some people wear a device to check. There is also medicine to treat diabetes.

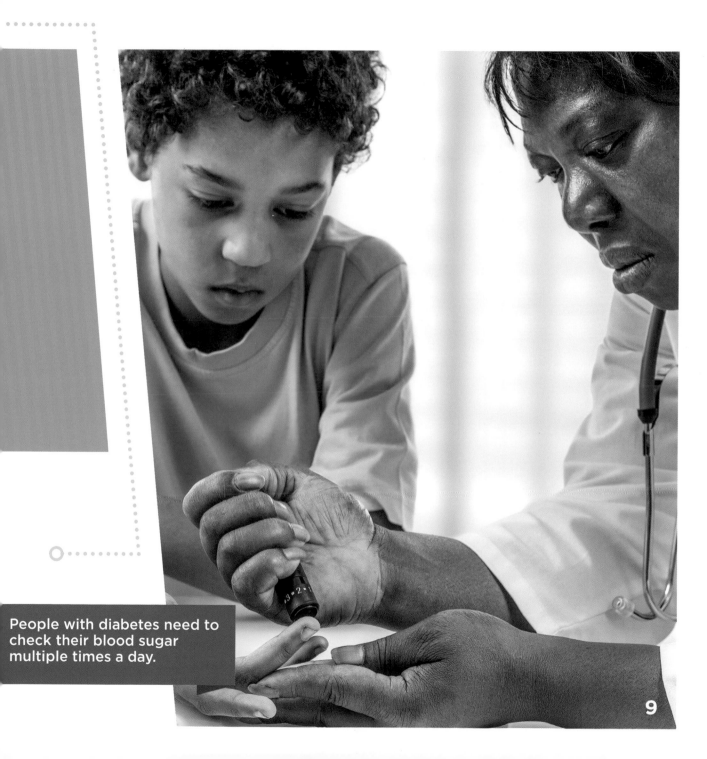

People with diabetes need to
check their blood sugar
multiple times a day.

These steps can help people with diabetes be healthier. Kids and grown-ups can have diabetes.

People may have big feelings about having a chronic illness. They may wonder what it means. They may wonder what may change. Their loved ones might have big feelings, too. These feelings are okay.

It's okay to have big feelings about chronic illnesses. You can still enjoy your loved one.

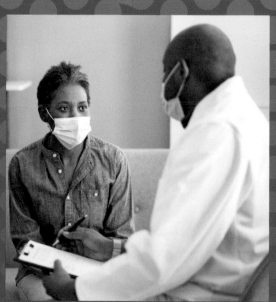

Having a chronic illness can cause **stress**. You might not be sure how to feel better. It can help to talk to someone about your worries.

Chronic illnesses are different for everyone. Some people can get treatment. Some people can get better quickly. Not every person can get better. It is not fair how that works.

Sometimes people with asthma use a machine called a nebulizer. It is a breathing treatment they can take at home.

Doctors or nurses can help.
Therapists and other care teams can help. There are many ways to help people with chronic illnesseses.

Look!

This kid is spending time with someone they love. They are finding ways to have fun together.

13

People with a chronic illness called celiac disease have an immune reaction to gluten in their body. They don't eat foods with wheat in them, like most breads.

LOVING SOMEOME WITH CHRONIC ILLNESS

Sometimes people we love get a chronic illness. Many people live a long time with one. People may die from a chronic illness. You might feel upset. You might feel sad or angry. It's okay to feel however you feel. It can be hard to love someone with a chronic illness.

Think!

Think about a chronic illness that you would like to learn more about. How could you learn more?

You can talk about your feelings. You can talk to your family and friends. Sometimes it helps to talk to a therapist. You could talk to someone with a chronic illness. It may help to talk to their loved ones.

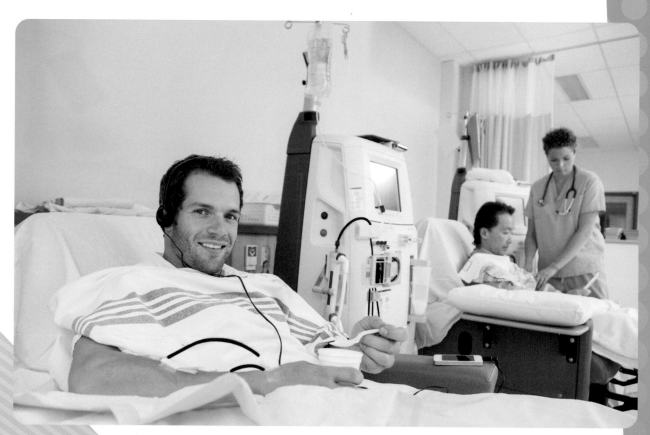

Someone with kidney disease can be treated with dialysis.

Loving someone with a chronic illness can be hard. Talking with someone you trust can be helpful.

17

SHOWING LOVE FOR OTHERS AND YOURSELF

You can show love for others. You can show love for yourself. You might not be able to help like you want. There are still many things you can try.

You might try doing the things you like to do.

You might focus on keeping yourself healthy and strong.

You might help your loved one with a chronic illness feel happy.

You might want to volunteer at places that help others.

You might decide to fight chronic illnesses when you're older.

It can be hard when a loved one has a chronic illness. Sometimes that might mean less attention is given to you.

You might have big feelings. You might want to find fun ways to help. You might ask a grown-up for special quality time.

Create!

Make a plan. Think of a fun day for a kid whose sibling has a chronic illness. What could be fun?

Ask Questions!

Ask a grown-up to help you learn. Ask what people are doing to help people with chronic illnesses. What good news can you find out?

Things to know:

Many people are working to help people with chronic illnesses. Scientists are learning what may cause chronic illnesses. They are trying to stop them from happening. Many treatments can help people. Helpers are finding ways to help kids with chronic illnesses.

Maybe you'll be one of the helpers one day. Maybe you already are.

21

GLOSSARY

Alzheimer's disease (ALZ-hie-muhrz dih-ZEEZ) a disease of the brain that affects memory; it happens mostly in older adults

asthma (AZ-muh) an illness that makes it hard to breathe

cancer (KAN-ser) when cells that are not normal grow and spread very fast

chronic fatigue syndrome (KRON-ik fuh-TEEG SIN-drohm) a long-term illness that affects many systems in the body; a symptom is extreme tiredness that doesn't go away with rest

diabetes (DYE-uh-BEE-teez) a chronic illness in which someone has too much sugar in their blood

fibromyalgia (FYE-broh-mye-AL-juh) a long-term health condition that causes pain and tenderness throughout the body

heart disease (HART dih-ZEEZ) a type of disease of the heart or blood vessels

hormone (HOR-mohn) a chemical in the body that acts like a messenger

insulin (IN-suh-lin) a hormone that helps control sugar and starch in the body

kidney disease (KID-nee dih-ZEEZ) a disease of the kidneys

stress (STREHS) the feeling of being worried and nervous

stroke STROHK) when part of your brain doesn't get enough blood flow

therapists (THAIR-uh-pists) professionals who help people work through their feelings and life challenges

LEARN MORE

Books:

How Many Marbles Do You Have?: Helping Children Understand the Limitations of Those with Chronic Fatigue Syndrome and Fibromyalgia by Melinda Malott

Living with a Chronic Illness - Jumo Health

Shia Learns About Insulin by Shaina Hatchell

Search online for the following video resource with an adult:
HiHo Kids - "Kids Meet a Teen with a Chronic Illness"

INDEX

ABOUT THE AUTHORS

Lacey Hilliard is a college professor, researcher, and parent. Her work is in understanding how grown-ups talk to children about the world around them. She particularly likes hearing what kids have to say about things.

AnneMarie McClain is an educator, researcher, and parent. Her work is about how kids and families can feel good about who they are. She especially loves finding ways to help kids and families feel seen in TV and books.